ROTATION

SNOW
BOARDING

LONDON, NEW YORK, MELBOURNE,
MUNICH, and DELHI

Created by Tall Tree Ltd
Consultant Tudor Thomas

For DK
Senior Designer/Brand Manager Lisa Lanzarini
Publishing Manager Simon Beecroft
Category Publisher Alex Allan
DTP Designer Hanna Ländin
Production Amy Bennett

First published in Great Britain in 2007 by
Dorling Kindersley Limited
80 Strand, London WC2R 0RL

A CIP catalogue for this book is available from the British Library.

ISBN 978-1-40531-836-5

High-resolution workflow proofed by Media Development and Printing Ltd, UK.
Printed and bound in China by Hung Hing Offset Printing Co, Ltd.

Discover more at

www.dk.com

SNOW BOARDING

Clive Gifford

Photographer Mark C Hopkins
Illustrator Des Higgins

CONTENTS

Snowboarders give each other **encouragement**. Here, an instructor congratulates a young boarder after nailing a trick.

A young snowboarder gets some air riding a slope in Sweden.

One of the great things about snowboarding is that it offers lots of variety. Whether you're experienced or just starting out, snowboarding constantly offers **new challenges** and new tricks to master.

ABOUT THIS BOOK

This book will tell you all about snowboarding. **It will help you learn the basics** – from how to stand up with your feet in the board bindings to performing carving turns. It will also show you some of the best **tricks** you can work towards.

Andreas, Calle, Markus, Wilma and Lisen chill out and pose for a photo.

INTRODUCTION

Snowboarding is an incredible, all-action sport.
Millions of snowboarders hit the slopes every year seeking excitement and adventure. Snowboarding lets you cruise slowly, carve downhill at speed or perform amazing acrobatic tricks and moves.

WE ALL AGREE SNOWBOARDING'S AWESOME!

MARKUS

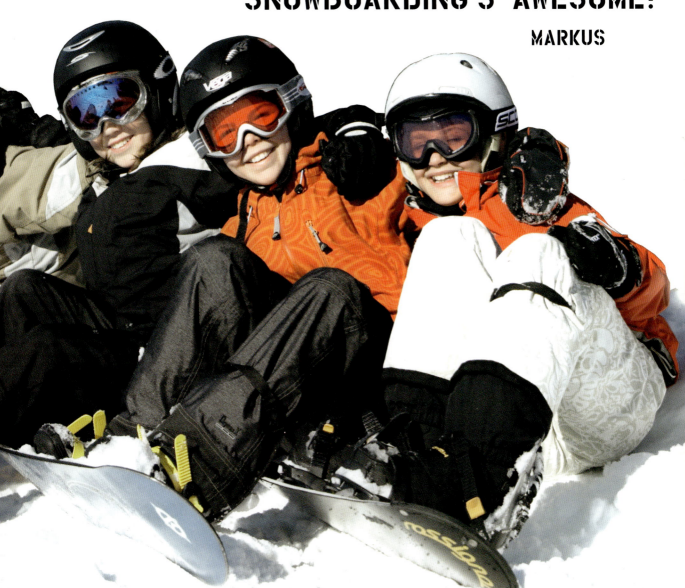

Ross gets incredible air in a high-jumping competition watched by hundreds of spectators and press photographers.

ROSS POWERS

Snowboarding joined the **Winter Olympics** in 1998 and Ross Powers was the first American to win an Olympic snowboarding medal in the **half-pipe** competition.

CLASSIC SNOWBOARDS

Snowboard design has changed a lot since the original Snurfer. One of Jake Burton's first designs, the Backhill, had reins like a toboggan, while Winterstick's Swallowtail had an unusual tail design to help ride new-fallen snow.

In the 1970s and early 1980s, the first **purpose** snowboards were developed by companies such as Burton and Winterstick. Today, there are dozens of other manufacturers, including K2 and Sims, that produce boards and clothing. They also sponsor top pro snowboarders.

SNURFER   BURTON BACKHILL   BURTON WOODY   SWALLOWTAIL

Terje pulls a superb grab during a freestyle competition. The Norwegian is one of the most famous of all snowboarders.

TERJE HAAKONSEN

One of the greatest-ever pro snowboarders is **Terje Haakonsen**. He first tried snowboarding on a **Swallowtail** board at age 13. Only four years later, he became world champion! He has won **five** world half-pipe championships.

OLD SCHOOL SNOWBOARDING

Snowboarding really began in the 1960s when Sherman Poppen built a **toy** for his children. He named it a **Snurfer** and in just one year – 1966 – he sold half a million! At the start, snowboarders were **banned** from many ski resorts, but today they are found in their millions at resorts all over the world.

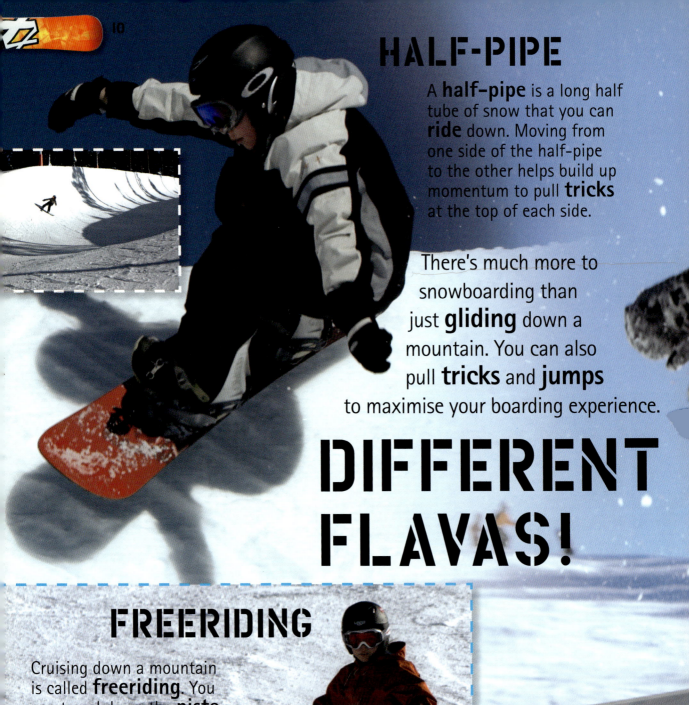

HALF-PIPE

A **half-pipe** is a long half tube of snow that you can **ride** down. Moving from one side of the half-pipe to the other helps build up momentum to pull **tricks** at the top of each side.

There's much more to snowboarding than just **gliding** down a mountain. You can also pull **tricks** and **jumps** to maximise your boarding experience.

DIFFERENT FLAVAS!

FREERIDING

Cruising down a mountain is called **freeriding**. You can travel down the **piste** using different types of turns, or sideslip down in a **falling leaf** pattern.

Wilma freeriding

Andreas pulls his knees up to his chest as he rises high with his board in mid-air.

I LOVE GETTING AIRBORNE

ANDREAS

FREESTYLE

Freestyle boarders jump off moguls, rails, benches... basically **anything** they can find. And if they can't find it, sometimes they'll **build** it.

GEARING UP

Snowboarding gear not only looks good. It keeps you **warm** and helps you stay **safe**. You wear layers of clothing, starting with a t-shirt, then a fleece and then an outer layer which is wind and waterproof. Put on your **helmet** and **goggles** and grab your **board** and you're ready for action.

Snowboarding's thirsty work! Drink water or juice regularly.

GETTING ALL THE GEAR
MAKES YOU LOOK
LIKE A PRO!

WILMA

STAYING WARM LOOKING GOOD

Staying **safe** and **warm** is essential, but you want to look **good** as well! Make sure you choose your **clothing** well, and take advice from a pro.

SUNSCREEN STOP YOUR GETTING BURNED.

JACKETS SHOULD LET YOU MOVE EASILY, BUT THEY SHOULD NOT BE TOO LOOSE.

Helmets are a **vital** part of any boarder's kit. Make sure that the chin strap is tightened **securely** so that the helmet will not move about.

TROUSERS NEED PADS TO STOP THEM FROM TEARING.

MAKE SURE YOUR BOOTS ARE COMFORTABLE.

I LIKE TO LOOK GOOD AND FEEL SAFE!

LISEN

BODY ARMOUR

As well as good **helmet**, you may want to invest in some more body protection. Special **back** padding is available to protect your **spine** and tail bone should you fall over backwards land heavily.

Good goggles **protect** your eyes from spraying snow and from the **glare** of the sun, which can cause **snow blindness**.

BOARD TIME

Snowboards come in lots of different types. **Freeride boards** are the most common. They have a longer nose than their tail. **Freestyle boards** are lighter and shorter than freeride boards. They can be ridden in either direction.

Boards come in lots of **designs**. Make sure that you pick a board to suit your **height** and the **style** you want to ride.

Look after your board, keep it **clean** and check the fittings are secure. **Waxing** the underside of the board regularly helps it to glide more smoothly.

SAFETY LEASH

A safety leash is a **strap** fitted to your board and your **front** leg. It stops your board running away when you are stepping into your bindings.

Make sure your leash is secure.

These boarders are ready to ride. Wilma holds her board up so that you can see its top surface, called the deck.

GOOFY is when you ride with your **right foot** as your front foot. See how the boarder (below right) leans so more of his weight is over his front foot.

REGULAR is when you ride with your **left foot** as your front foot. This boarder (below left) keeps his head up and is looking ahead.

Riding goofy

STANCE

Try to keep your **back** straight and turn your hips and shoulders so that you face the direction you're **travelling**. Hold your arms out to balance.

Riding regular

BINDINGS

Bindings come in different types. Some **lock** when you step into them, but most use heel and toe **straps** to hold you in place. Learn how your bindings work and practise putting your feet into them.

1 Start by placing your board on flat ground or across a slope – not pointing downhill. Clip on your safety leash.

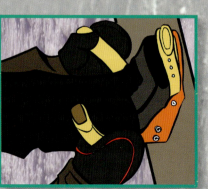

2 Put your front foot into the binding. Push your heel back and tighten the heel strap.

Try to keep your knees slightly bent, so they can absorb some of the bumps as you ride.

BINDINGS AND STANCE

Bindings are **fittings** on the deck which join you and your boots to your **board**. Ask your **instructor** to help you set them up on your board. Your stance should be **comfortable** to let you ride well and perform all your moves.

3 Tighten the toe strap and stand up. To stop yourself moving, dig the board's edge into the snow.

4 Now slip into your back binding and tighten the straps. Make sure all straps are secure. You're now on board!

MY INSTRUCTOR WAS BRILLIANT.
I WAS RIDING AND
TURNING IN NO TIME.

CALLE

SNOWTIME!

Geared up and on board? Now's the time to hit the slopes! If you're new to snowboarding, signing up to a snowboarding school is a brilliant idea. **Getting lessons** from an experienced instructor is the very best way to get started. You'll meet other beginners too.

This is the way to **carry** a snowboard when you're walking around. Tuck both hands underneath the board and carry it **behind** your back, level to the ground.

SLOPECRAFT

Getting to the slopes or a fun park is exciting. But **always** keep your eyes and ears open, **follow instructions** on signs and be aware of other snowboarders nearby.

GETTING ONTO A T-BAR LIFT

1 With your front foot in its binding and your board pointing up the slope, wait for the T-bar lift to arrive.

2 Grab hold of the T-bar firmly and get your back foot on your board. Place the T-bar between your legs.

3 Grip the handle with both hands. Keep your knees flexed. Try not to lean forward too much.

GETTING OFF A CHAIRLIFT

With just your front foot in its bindings, get ready to **dismount** a chairlift. Point your board forwards with the nose tilted **up** a little. Set the tail of your board down first, before standing up.

ENJOY THE RIDE UP ON A CHAIRLIFT. YOU GET AWESOME VIEWS!

MARKUS

Push off with **both** hands and glide away from the **unloading area**, keeping an eye out for other snowboarders nearby.

Keep your board nice and **flat** so it doesn't **catch** on its edge.

I USE PUSHING OFF TO GET ME AROUND A FUN PARK.

LISEN

1 Get your front foot into its binding. Stand upright and put your weight over your front foot.

2 Push against the ground with your back foot, making contact just behind your front foot.

3 As you start moving, place your back foot onto the deck. Use your arms to help keep your balance.

PUSHING OFF

A terrific way of getting going is to practise **pushing off**. It's like pushing a skateboard along with one foot on the **deck** and the other foot moving you forwards. To practise pushing off, choose a piece of **level ground** or an area that slopes upwards slightly. As with all practice runs, make sure that the way is **clear** ahead of you.

Walk up a **slope** with your foot still in its binding. Face the hill and pull the board up **behind** you as you walk. Keep the board positioned **across** the slope.

Try small, gentle push-offs at first. Then gradually build up to longer glides.

Your back foot is placed **between** the two **bindings** as you glide.

FALLING SIDEWAYS

As you fall to the **side**, try to keep your arms tucked in. Land on your **knees** and roll onto your shoulder and back to spread out the **impact** of the fall.

FALLING SAFELY

Wrists get injured more than any other part of your body in snowboarding. So **never** stick your hands out when falling. Instead, **bunch** them into fists and try to fall on your forearms. When falling backwards, **collapse** your legs and keep your body **relaxed**. Land on your bottom and roll back to cushion the fall.

BOTH FEET FORWARD

Sitting in the snow is all part of snowboarding whether you're taking a **rest** or you've fallen. This means that you'll spend lots of time **getting up** off the floor with both boots in your bindings. But with the right technique you can be **up** and **away** in just a few seconds.

STANDING UP

1 With your heel edge in the snow and your board across the slope, inch towards the snowboard.

2 Push up with your hands and start to straighten your knees. Keep your weight over the heel edge of the board.

3 Get a friend to help you balance and stand up when you first start snowboarding.

FACING THE WRONG WAY?

1 If you are facing the snow, you're on the toe edge. To switch to the heel edge, dip one shoulder and roll onto it.

2 Twist at your waist and lift your legs up high enough to get your board clear of the snow.

3 Complete your roll and you'll find yourself the right way round.

HEELSIDE

To sideslip **heelside**, start by positioning your board across the slope so that your **toeside** edge faces downhill. Lift your toes and dig the heel edge of your board into the snow to keep it still. Lower your toes and tilt the board a little towards the toe edge to start moving. Tilt back a little to dig the heel edge in again to slow or stop.

1 To heelslip, let the board glide downhill, keeping your knees bent and your weight over both feet.

2 Slow down by putting more weight over the heelside of your board.

Keep your back straight as you head downhill.

Keep your knees bent to absorb any little bumps.

Make sure your first sideslipping moves take place on a gentle slope with an instructor or experienced snowboarder to help you.

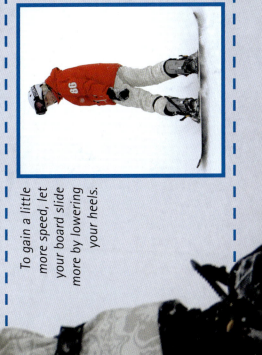

To gain a little more speed, let your board slide more by lowering your heels.

TOESIDE SLIPPING

In **toeside** slipping, you travel down the slope **back** first. Balance on the balls of your feet. To control your speed, raise your heels. This helps the **toe edge** of your snowboard bite into the snow to act like a brake.

SIDESLIPPING

Sideslipping is the first way **beginners** learn to ride down a slope. You travel downhill with your weight spread **evenly** over both feet and your board facing **across** the slope. Digging in or releasing one of the **side edges** of your board helps you to control the speed of the board. You can **sideslip** on either the heelside or toeside edges of your board.

ALWAYS KEEP THE EDGE FACING DOWNHILL UP AND OUT OF THE SNOW.

LISEN

SLIDE AWAY

The key with **linking** your sliding moves is to start nice and slow and gently **alter** the pressure on the board. Feel how the board **reacts** to you putting a little more **pressure** on the heelside and on the toeside.

Before travelling down a slope, study its features and plot out the best route to get you to the bottom.

1 At the start of your run, ease more pressure onto your front foot. The board will start to move in that direction.

2 As you start to move, gradually even out the pressure over both feet. This will cause the board to slow.

3 Just before the board slows to a stop, put more pressure onto your back foot to change direction.

In falling leaf turns, you move down a slope from one side to the other.

YOU CAN USE THE FALLING LEAF TO GET ALL THE WAY DOWN A SLOPE.

WILMA

FALLING LEAF TURNS

You can **link** your **toeside** and **heelside** sliding moves together. Done well, these will see you travel gently back and forth across and down a slope. The pattern you make is like a leaf falling in **autumn**, hence its name.

4 Change the direction you are looking in. With more pressure over your back foot, you will start to move in that direction, taking you back across the slope.

5 As you start to move back across the slope, even out the pressure over both feet to slow the board.

6 To continue the falling leaf pattern and switch directions, keep alternating the pressure from front to back as you cross the slope.

TURN AND BURN

The falling leaf pattern helps you to turn in a simple way. But to really get moving around the slopes you need to learn other types of turns. **Carving turns** let you change direction really sharply and at quite fast speeds. **Heelside** and **toeside turns** and carving turns are vital both on the slopes and in freestyle terrain such as half-pipes.

LEARNING TOE AND HEELSIDE TURNS ROCK. NOW I CAN TRAVEL EVERYWHERE!

MARKUS

ALWAYS LOOK
IN THE DIRECTION YOU WANT TO HEAD!

LISEN

SLIDE IT
ROUND

To perform a toeside turn, you need to **lead** with the front foot and gently adjust the pressure on the **toe** edge of your board. Keeping your weight off the back foot helps let the tail slide and drift round **behind** you. Try to complete a turn so that it starts to take you back **up** the slope. You should come to a gentle halt.

Keep your knees bent and head up.

1 Build up a gentle speed. Lean forwards over your front foot.

2 Lift your heels slightly and put pressure on the toeside edge of your board.

Lisen's weight is over the toe edge of her board as she makes a toeside turn.

3 Don't lean back but turn your hips and shoulders in the direction of the turn to help ease the board round.

TOESIDE TURN

You've learned to change direction by **slipping** across the slope. Now you're ready for real turns. You create turns by putting different amounts of **pressure** on different parts of your board. Practise these on really gentle slopes and in plenty of **space** without other boarders or skiers in the way. As you get better you can increase your **speed** and the sharpness of the turn.

HEELSIDE TURN

The heelside turn is similar to the toeside turn but with the **turning action** taking place on the heel edge of your snowboard. As with the toeside turn, you need to get the board **running flat** on the snow before applying pressure to the edge of your board. Once you can perform both heelside and toeside turns, try to link them together. With linked turns under **control**, you will be able to cruise the slopes freely.

Lisen performs a smooth heelside turn. See how her weight is over the heel edge of the board with the toe edge slightly off the ground.

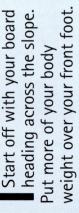

Start off with your board heading across the slope. Put more of your body weight over your front foot.

DOs AND DON'Ts

Do keep your knees **bent,** your head **up** and your back nice and straight throughout the **turn.** Do keep your body movements smooth and gentle. Don't **jerk** your body or put your weight on the back foot. Don't stick your bottom out and go **up** on your heels as you make the turn.

HEELSIDE TURNS ARE HARDER THAN TOESIDE TURNS SO BE PATIENT!

LISEN

When you have turned the amount you want to, lower your toes and ease off the heel edge. This should get your board level and running flat on the snow.

Your knees should be flexed so that you can adjust your position quickly.

4 Keep your weight over your front foot and pressure on the heel edge.

2 The nose will point down the slope. Start to put pressure on your heel edge.

3 Turn your body into the turn. The board's tail should start sliding downhill.

38

HEELSIDE CARVE

A heelside carve uses the **heelside** edge of your board to turn on the slope. As with other turns, the secret to performing this move is to **transfer** your weight to different parts of the board.

1 With your weight over both feet, lean back over the heelside edge of your board. You should feel the edge grip the snow and bring you round in the turn.

2 To end your carving turn, straighten up your body and push up from the **heel edge** of the board to get it running flat on the snow.

CARVING

See how the board is right on the toe edge as it turns.

The turns so far use the **base** of your board to skid or slide round. Carving is **different** and **exciting**. It uses the **edges** of your board to make turns in the snow. Carving turns take lots of practice and you need to be travelling at a good **speed**.

By staying on the **edges** of your board and leaning into each turn, you can link **carving** turns into sweeping moves across a slope.

TOESIDE CARVE

Travel across a slope on the **heelside** edge of your board. Roll your board onto the **toeside** edge as you turn your shoulders into the direction of the turn. Bend your **knees** and lean into the turn but keep your back straight.

Keep your back straight and look in the direction of the turn.

START YOUR CARVING ON GENTLE SLOPES AND BE PREPARED FOR FALLS!

CALLE

Bend your knees as you lean into the turn.

EXTREME CARVE

Top snowboarders who **shred** up a slope by travelling really fast can lean so low and hard into a **carving** turn that their hand brushes the snow's surface.

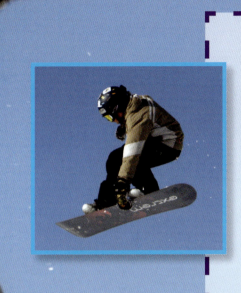

FREESTYLE FUN

Once you've mastered and linked your **turns** together, you can freeride the slopes of your resort all day. But many snowboarders want more. They want to perform **tricks** such as jumps, slides, spins and grabs. **Freestyle** tricks can take lots of time to master so don't give up if you don't nail a trick at first.

THE HARDER THE TRICK, THE MORE RESPECT YOU EARN FOR NAILING IT.

MARKUS

TAIL WHEELIE

To pull a **wheelie**, get moving in a straight line. Straighten your **front** leg and bend your back leg. Start to lean back and **lift** your front leg a little.

The nose of your board should rise off the ground. Lean forwards to get the board back on the snow.

Keep your head up and your arms out. Your front leg stays straight as you wheelie.

As you get more confident, try a more aggressive lean backwards – but watch out that you don't topple over. See how long you can keep this wheelie going.

STATIC 180

This move can help you **flip** direction quickly. Make sure you practise it on a piece of **flat ground** first. Then, when you've got more confidence, try it out while you're moving.

KEEP WORKING AT IT UNTIL YOU NAIL IT. IT'S A GREAT MOVE!
MARKUS

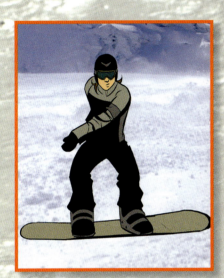

1 Bend your knees and twist your body in the opposite direction from the one you want to turn in.

2 Spring upwards, lifting your knees up to bring the board up off the ground. Twist your body in the direction you want to turn.

3 As you turn 180 degrees, hold your arms out for balance. Try to land on the whole of your board, with knees bent.

SIMPLE TRICKS

There are enough snowboarding **tricks** around to keep you amused for years and years. Start out **simple** and nail these two tricks. They can both help you with more **advanced** tricks you might tackle later. Always work on new tricks in a flat or gently sloping area.

AN OLLIE OFF A JUMP GETS YOU BIG AIR TIME TO PULL OTHER TRICKS.

CALLE

Just like in skateboarding, the **Ollie** is a simple **jumping move** you can do on flat ground or to clear a small obstacle like a tree branch or mogul. Mastering this move is the **first big step** towards nailing other great tricks such as mid-air grabs of your board.

THE OLLIE

1 Ride at low to medium speed and shift your weight to your back foot. Crouch down a little and then spring up, pulling your front foot up first.

2 Jump off your back foot, using the tail of the board as a spring. Pull both knees up towards your body to lift the board.

3 Level out once in the air. Bend your knees as you land to cushion the impact, and spread your weight so you can ride away balanced.

FRONTSIDE GRAB

To perform a **frontside grab** during an Ollie, you need to be quick. Once in the air, reach down and **grab** the frontside of your board. Use your other arm to keep you balanced.

NOSE GRAB

Grab and release the nose before the board levels out and gets close to landing.

You can use an Ollie to get even **more air** when flying off a ramp or ridge. If you get plenty of air, try out a **nose grab**. Keeping your head up, stretch forwards with your front arm and use your fingers to grab the board's nose.

360 SPIN

3 The board starts to level out in the air.

2 As he twists, the boarder performs a grab.

This boarder is performing a full **360** spin in mid-air. With all spins, you wind up your body in the **opposite** direction to the turn, then uncoil and **spin** your body round. Try to look over your shoulder in the **direction** that you are turning.

4 The boarder focuses on where he wants to land.

IN A SPIN

Spins are moves in the air where you rotate or turn. They are measured in degrees, so a **180** is spinning in half a complete circle and a **360** is spinning all the way round. **Advanced** snowboarders who are really good at tricks may even be able to perform a type of somersault in the air, called a **flip**.

START WITH SMALL SPINS AND BUILD UP TO 180s, 360s OR MORE!

ANDREAS

I The boarder launches off a ramp. He's turning to his right.

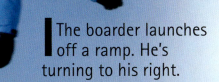

BACK FLIP

This is a spectacular trick move for **advanced** snowboarders only.

I. Hit a jump at speed and bend your knees to gain as much height as possible.

2. Throw your body back and extend your legs so you rotate in the air.

3. Spot a landing point as early as possible and try to keep your balance when you hit the slope.

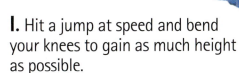

FUN PARKS

Fun parks, or terrain parks, are heaven for freestyle snowboarders. They usually consist of lots of different features you can **pull moves** on linked by areas of flat or gently sloping snow. Terrain park features include **jumps** and **half-pipes** that you can ride in, as well as table tops, rails and platforms that you can slide your board along.

SNOW PARKS ARE GREAT FUN AND CHALLENGING.

ANDREAS

I LEARNED A GREAT NEW TRICK FROM MY FRIENDS AT A PARK TODAY!

MARKUS

Slides are basic moves performed along rails or fun boxes. You can slide on a rail with your board pointing along it. This is called a **50-50 slide**. Other slides include the **boardslide** where your board is across the rail balanced between your two feet.

BOARDSLIDE

1 Approach the rail at a medium speed and ride up onto the rail. Land your board on the rail midway between the bindings.

2 Keep your board flat as it slides along the rail. Try to keep your body straight and your weight balanced over the board.

3 As you approach the end of the rail, lift your knees up to jump off the rail. Spin the board back 90 degrees before you land.

NOSE SLIDE TO FAKIE

Ollie up onto the rail

Nose slide along the rail

Dismount riding fakie

Some boxes and rails are sited above the ground so snowboarders have to perform an **Ollie** to land on them. This snowboarder is on a rail performing a nose slide. His weight is on his front foot to keep the nose on the rail. He **dismounts** with the tail of the board leading and rides away fakie.

FUN PARK TRICKS

Fun parks can be **daunting** at first. Watch others and pick up **tips** before trying out some simple moves yourself. Be **patient** and wait your turn and, once you've ridden a rail, platform or pipe, **get clear** so that others can have a go.

BOXES AND RAILS

Once you've managed to ride a straight rail or **fun box**, try out some of the other features found in the fun park. **Rainbow boxes** are fun to ride even if you're quite new to snowboarding. **C-rails** are a tougher prospect and best left until you have more experience.

C-RAIL

Once on the rail, the snowboarder gets his body weight over the foot directly above the rail to stay balanced.

He looks ahead to the point he plans to land once he hops off the rail.

3 The boarder brings his board back straight using his arms to balance.

This boarder is riding a **C-rail** which is a rail shaped in a curve and angled down **towards** the ground. The boarder gets onto the rail by performing a jump after approaching at **medium** speed.

The boarder heads off the box and onto the snow.

RAINBOW BOX

A rainbow box is a gently curving **hump** sticking out of the snow. They're found at many **fun parks**. You can ride these in many different ways including **straight** up and over or, as here, by skewing your board at an **angle** at the top.

2 The boarder rotates the board round to ride the top of the box at an angle.

I The boarder rides straight up the box, keeping his body weight slightly forwards.

I LOVE TRYING OUT DIFFERENT BOXES, RAILS AND RAMPS. IT'S COOL!

CALLE

Calle turns at the top of a half-pipe.

This experienced snowboarder gets some air above the top of a half-pipe.

THE HALF-PIPE

A half-pipe consists of a **flat floor** with curved **transitions** that lead to vertical **walls** on either side. The whole of the half-pipe slopes downhill.

Wilma prepares to drop into a half-pipe.

HALF-PIPES LOOK SCARY BUT THEY'RE AWESOME TO RIDE.

WILMA

RIDING A HALF-PIPE

Half-pipes are large, U-shaped trenches **dug** out of the snow. They're the big attraction at many **fun parks** but they're tough to master. Make sure you are experienced at snowboarding on **regular** slopes first. Get a feel for the half-pipe by gently riding back and forth straight across the **lower parts** of a pipe. Once you've got some experience, you can try **dropping in** from the top.

DROPPING IN

Entering a half-pipe from the top is called **dropping in**. Place your board over the pipe lip and move gently forwards. Don't lean backwards as you travel down the **wall** of the pipe. It is important that you wait your turn in a half-pipe and don't try to push in.

HALF-PIPE TRICKS

After riding the **flat floor** and **transitions** of a half-pipe gently, you'll want to work your way up the pipe's **walls**. You need to be able to turn near the top of the walls so that you can head back down the slope after each hit. You can **slide turn** or, if you're really experienced, perform a **frontside air** move.

To perform this simple slide and hop turn, get on the **toeside** edge of your board as you begin your turn into the wall. Bring your **knees** up to lift the board off the wall, performing a small hop. Turn your **head** to look back into the pipe and twist your hips to help bring your board around. Your board should land on the **heelside** edge as you head back down the pipe.

FRONTSIDE AIR

1. The speed of the board carries you over the lip.
2. Bring your knees up to your chest and grab the board.
3. Turn in the air.
4. Land heading down the pipe with knees bent.

Andreas performs a textbook frontside air.

ABOVE THE LIP

This **spectacular** turn takes place above the lip of the half-pipe. It's for **experienced** snowboarders only. You ride up the wall quite fast but under control. The speed of the board will carry it above the lip of the half-pipe. Pull your knees up to your chest. Grab the toeside edge of the board with your **front hand**. You must turn the board 180 degrees in the air. Look over your shoulder to where you want to **land** and, as you start coming down, let go of the board and prepare for landing.

BACKCOUNTRY

Some experienced snowboarders go **backcountry** – exploring areas of hills and mountains which are not part of a resort. Boarding backcountry can be extremely dangerous.

SNOWBOARD RACING

Snowboard racing is often against the clock, racing straight downhill or zig-zagging between gates in a slalom. Boardercross pits four to six boarders together in a race over obstacles.

Four boardercrossers speed down the slopes, carving around a gate.

GOING PRO

So you think you're pretty good now at **snowboarding**? But you still have a way to go before you can become a **pro**. The top **pro** snowboarders compete in lots of different major competitions including the X Games and Winter Olympics. To be as good as them, you will need to **practise** really, really hard as often as you can.

CROWD PLEASERS

Freestyle competitions draw **huge** crowds who watch spectacular jumps (or aerials) off ramps and amazing half-pipe tricks. Here, a crowd of more than **20,000** people flock to watch pro snowboarders at the Innsbruck Air and Style Competition.

SHAUN WHITE

Top pro snowboarder **Shaun White** is nicknamed the "Flying Tomato" because of his **red** hair and his spectacular aerial moves. He won a snowboarding **gold** medal at the 2006 Winter Olympics in Turin, Italy.

IN THE KNOW

Snowboarding is great fun but it can be dangerous. Always ride **marked slopes** and never stray **off-piste** where there might be a risk of an **avalanche** or **hazards** like cliffs or steep drops. Learn what the **signs** and routes mean at your resort and always **obey** rules. They're not designed to spoil your fun, they're made to keep you safe.

SAFETY SIGNALS

ALL OK!

STOP!

Always snowboard with others, so that if one of you **falls** and gets hurt, someone else can get **help**. Hand signals can be a clear way to let others know whether you need help.

GLOSSARY

AIRS Jumps off the ground on a snowboard.

BACKSIDE When a trick or turn is executed with the snowboarder's back facing the obstacle.

BASE The underside of a snowboard.

BINDING The device that locks your boot to your snowboard.

CARVE To ride fast curves using the edges of your snowboard.

DECK The top flat surface of a snowboard.

DROP OR DROP IN To take your turn down a slope or to enter a half-pipe from the top.

FAKIE Riding your snowboard backwards from your normal stance.

FRONTSIDE When a trick or turn is performed with the snowboarder's front facing the ramp or obstacle.

FUN BOX A box-like feature in a fun park. It is usually wider than a rail and is raised just above the snow.

GOOFY STANCE Snowboarding with your right foot as your front foot.

GRAB Using your hand or hands to hold your board during a move.

HANDPLANT A half-pipe trick where the boarder performs a handstand on one or both hands.

HEELSIDE TURN A turn made on the heelside edge of your snowboard.

INVERT Any trick in which the snowboarder turns upside down in the air.

LIP The top edge of a half-pipe.

MOGULS Bumps in the snow.

OFF-PISTE Any slope away from a marked trail or run.

OLLIE A jumping move where the snowboarder pulls their board into the air.

PISTE A groomed area of snow marked out and prepared for snowboarders or skiers.

POWDER Deep snow that usually has just fallen.

REGULAR STANCE Snowboarding with your left foot as your front foot.

SAFETY LEASH A strap between the snowboard and the snowboarder's front leg that stops the snowboard from sliding away.

SIDESLIP To travel down a slope sideways with the length of the board across the slope.

SLALOM A timed race through a series of poles or gates.

STANCE How your feet and body are positioned on your snowboard.

TOESIDE TURN A turn made using the toeside edge of your snowboard.

INDEX

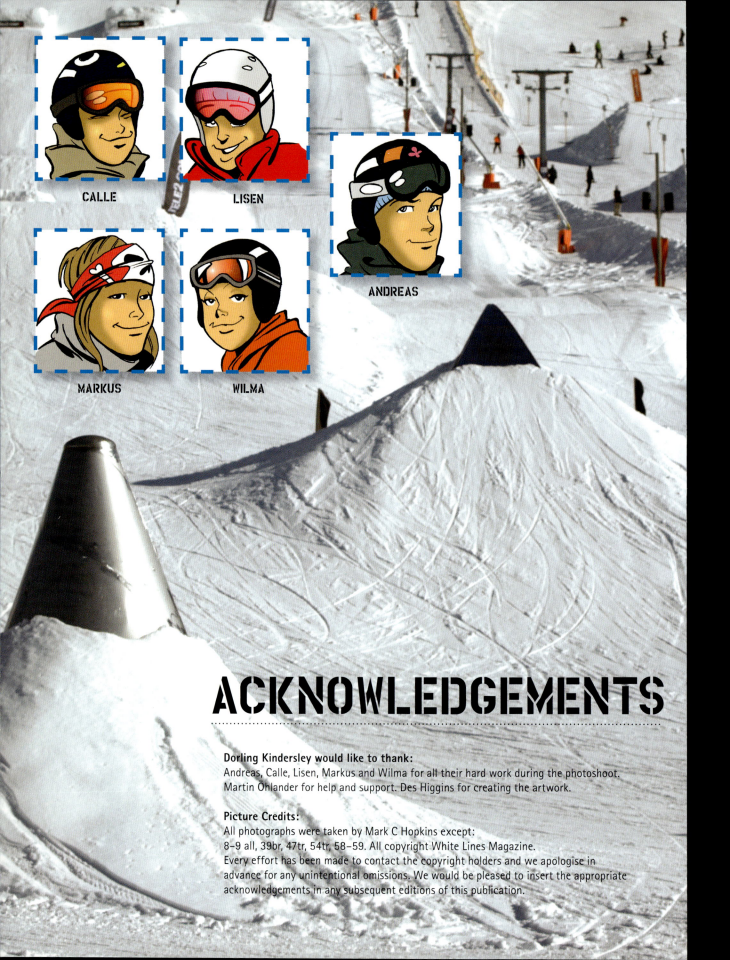

CALLE

LISEN

ANDREAS

MARKUS

WILMA

ACKNOWLEDGEMENTS

Dorling Kindersley would like to thank:
Andreas, Calle, Lisen, Markus and Wilma for all their hard work during the photoshoot.
Martin Öhlander for help and support. Des Higgins for creating the artwork.

Picture Credits:
All photographs were taken by Mark C Hopkins except:
8–9 all, 39br, 47tr, 54tr, 58–59. All copyright White Lines Magazine.
Every effort has been made to contact the copyright holders and we apologise in
advance for any unintentional omissions. We would be pleased to insert the appropriate
acknowledgements in any subsequent editions of this publication.